Light

Written by Maria Gordon
and
Illustrated by Mike Gordon

Wayland

Simple Science

Air
Colour
Day and Night
Heat
Electricity and Magnetism
Float and Sink

Light
Materials
Push and Pull
Rocks and Soil
Skeletons and Movement
Sound

Series Editor: Catherine Baxter
Advice given by: Audrey Randall - member of the Science Working Group for the National Curriculum.

First published in 1994 by
Wayland (Publishers) Ltd
61 Western Road, Hove
East Sussex, BN3 1JD, England

© Copyright 1994 Wayland (Publishers) Ltd

British Library Cataloguing in Publication Data
Gordon, Maria
  Light. - (Simple Science Series)
  I. Title II. Gordon, Mike III. Series 535

ISBN 0-7502-1289-6

Typeset by Liz Miller, Wayland (Publishers) Ltd
Printed and bound in Italy by G Canale

Contents

What is light?	4
Where does light come from?	5
Light bulbs	10
How does light travel?	12
Reflection	14
Light and colour	20
See-through things	24
Shadows	26
Plants and light	28
Notes for adults	30
Other books to read	31
Index	32

Light is a sort of energy. We call it energy because it makes things happen...

Light helps us to see. It helps plants grow. Light can burn things - even our skin.

Most of the light around us is made by the Sun. It is dark at night because there is no light from the Sun. So we have to use light from other things.

What things can you see here that make light?

Which are the ones that people have made?

Long ago, cave people made light with fire.
Some burnt animal fat in bowls.

Later people used candles and lamps. These worked by burning wax, oil or gas.

Now we have light-bulbs. They were invented by Thomas Edison. It may surprise you to hear that his teacher didn't think he was clever!

Many bulbs have a long, curly wire inside them which gets very hot and shines. Now there are also bulbs which have paint or gas inside them which glows.

Light is moving all the time. It travels very fast. In fact, in the time it takes to say 'Wonderwoman', it could go eight times around the Earth.

Light travels in straight lines. In a dark room, shine a small torch down a straight straw. What happens?

Now bend the straw. What happens?

Although light travels in straight lines, when it hits things, it bounces off them a bit like a ball. This is called reflection.

Find a mirror, some shiny stones, white and coloured paper and some bicycle safety bands. Make a room dark. Shine a torch on the things you have found. Which ones reflect the most light?

Look in a mirror. Light bounces off you and on to the mirror.
The mirror bounces back the light so well that you can see your face in it.

What other things make reflections you can see? What happens if the reflectors are curved or if they are smooth?

Did you know the Moon does not make light? It shines because it is reflecting the Sun's light.

At night we cannot see the Sun, but it is still shining. Sunlight is falling on the other side of the world and on the Moon. They both reflect the Sun's light.

When things do not reflect light they are soaking it up. Black things look black because they soak up all the light that hits them.

White things look white because they reflect most of the light that hits them.

White light is made up of lots of colours!

Rainbows happen when something makes the colours in white light spread out.

Raindrops can make light spread out. Can you think of other things that do this? (The pictures will help you!)

Try jumbling colours
to make white light.
Make a disc
like this.

Push a pencil
through the middle.

Watch what happens
when you spin the disc.

There are lots of things that you can see straight through. We say these things are transparent. Light goes through them.

Some things, like water and curved glass, let light through but make it turn.

Stand a straw in a glass of water. The light turning makes the straw look as if it is bent.

Can light go through YOU? Face a light (but do not look straight at it). Now look at the ground behind you. Is some of it darker than the ground in front? What shape is on the darker ground?

The dark shapes are called shadows.

Make shadows with different objects and lights.

Plants soak up light and use it to make food. Without light, plants die.

Look at these pictures.
How many different ways can you see light being used?

Notes for adults

The Simple Science series helps children to reach Key Stage 1: Attainment targets 1-4 of the Science National Curriculum. Below are some suggestions to help complement and extend the learning in this book.

4/5 Sample and discuss the importance of sunscreens and shades. Research sun worship in history.

6/7 Find the three natural light sources in the pictures. Compare the brightness and the heat of the different sources.

8/9 What lights are used in different countries today?

10/11 Research Humphrey Davy (British 1778-1829). Why do bulbs join up to wires? Make charts of bulb types and quantities used at home/in school.

12/13 Sunlight travels to Earth. Because it spreads out, how much reaches other planets?

14/15 Think of examples of things that sparkle or glow. Investigate safety in the dark eg safety bands. Use a decorative fibre optic lamp to show that light bounces back and forth inside the curving fibres.

16/17 Bounce light from mirrors. Investigate mirrors in lighthouses, cameras, etc. Read the Greek myth of Medusa.

18/19 Draw moon shapes. Use a telescope. Read *The Moon in the Mill Pond* from 'Nights With Uncle Remus' by J. C. Harris.
20/21 Lay out different coloured socks in the sun. The socks that feel the warmest have absorbed the most sunlight.
22/23 Paint with rainbow colours. Write rainbow poems.
24/25 Research jellyfish and catfish. Investigate lenses and coloured glass.
26/27 Experiment with multiple light sources. What happens when you shine two torches at a ball (see illustration)? Put on shadow plays. Draw round shadows. Make silhouettes. Read ghost stories.
28/29 Compare light deprived and normal plant/seed growth. Discuss food chains. Research light used in religion. Go to a laser show!

Other books to read

Light by K. Davies and W. Oldfield (Wayland, 1991)
Light by Ralph Chase (Blackwell Education, 1990)
Light by Chris Oxlade (Watts, 1993)
Light & Dark *Into Science* series (Oxford Primary Books, 1994)

Index

animals 29

candles 9

cave people 8

Edison, Thomas 10

energy 4

gas 9, 11

glass 25

lightbulbs 10

mirrors 16

moon 18

oil 9

plants 4, 28-29

rainbows 22

reflection 14, 17, 18-20

shadows 26-27

sun 5

torch 13

water 25

wax 9